Break Free

Lelanie Gongon

Presentation by *BookLeaf Publishing*

Web: www.bookleafpub.com

E-mail: info@bookleafpub.com

ISBN:9789358314793

First edition 2024

ACKNOWLEDGEMENT

It was always my dream to see my name written on the front cover of a book. Until one day, an opportunity showed up in my social media account about a 21-day challenge to write poems and to be published as a book. Without any second thought, I took the chance and here I am now sharing my book with you all.

In this book are my unspoken thoughts and emotions that I had hidden within me for years. Inspired by my past experiences, present desires and future dreams built together with my loved ones, family and friends from past and present encounters. They are the reasons for who I am today and who I dream of being someday. May you enjoy reading my poems and have a glimpse of my life journeys. Hoping I will inspire someone to have the courage to break free and follow their heart.

Table of Contents

Healing a Broken Heart...................................... 1

Don't Know What to Do..................................... 3

Anxious Mind...5

Blocked Emotions.. 7

Listen to Your Heart..................................... 9

Worth the Wait?...11

One More Chance..13

If Meant to Be.. 15

Unsent Message... 17

Cherished Memories....................................19

Just Keep Showing Up..................................21

I Will Be Over You Someday.................... 23

Rock Bottom..25

One Step at A Time.................................. 27

She Had Been Through Enough...................... 28

She Chose to Live Her Life Than to Worry.......30

Heal Your Heart...32

Genuine Forgiveness................................. 33

I Am Where I Am, And It's Okay..................... 35

Beyond Your Wildest Dream........................... 37

Let Go and Break Free................................ 39

Wait Patiently.. 41

New Beginnings.. 42

Unconditional Love.................................... 43

Live Without Regrets..................................45

Those Little Things................................ 46

Like A Diamond....................................47

Lost Opportunity..................................48

Karma..49

Right Directions....................................50

How I wish I Can..................................51

Love Yourself..................................... 53

Magnetic Attraction..............................54

Stop Comparing Yourself......................55

Am I Over You?..................................56

We Don't Know................................ 57

Divine Timing.................................. 58

Unfold Naturally................................59

With Gratitude.................................. 60

And I Waited.................................... 61

Wishing I Am Near Your Side................ 62

Treat Yourself Better.......................... 64

You've Got This............................... 65

Speak Your Mind..............................66

Hope I Know....................................67

Are You Ready?................................68

Limiting Beliefs................................69

Opposites Attract.............................. 70

When Things Start to Fall Into Place...........71

You Are Enough................................ 72

Invisible String Attached...................... 73

Lead Me The Way.............................. 75

Just Because.................................. 76

Open Your Heart.............................. 77

Breaking to Breakthrough.................. 78

Healing a Broken Heart

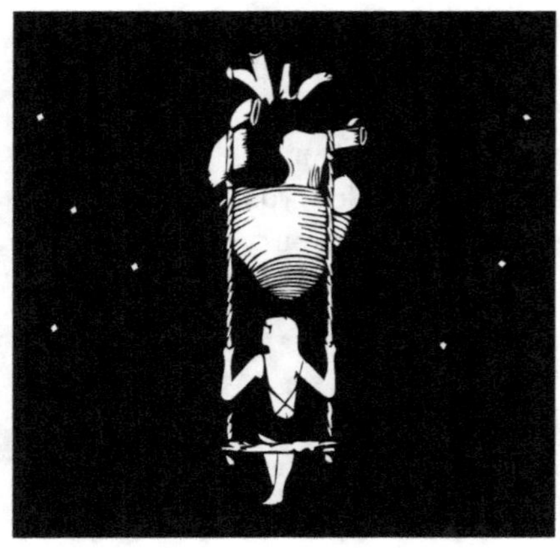

Keeping all the hurts,
Faking a smile,
Keep trying to go on daily life,
While hiding all this pain.

Here I am again,
For a countless time,
Curing my heart aches,
Showing up even if I am tired.

What have I done to deserve this?
What do I have to tell you?
What do you want me to do?
What do you want me to say?

Why I still love you,
Even if you keep on walking away?
Why do you have to block me,
And keep on pushing me away?

How can I forget you?
How can I stop loving you?
My heart wants to follow you.
All I want is to be with you.

What shall I do now?
How shall I move on?
Do I take the path far away?
Shall I take the opposite way?

I am too confused,
I don't know what to do.
You ask me to be patient,
But how long will I wait?

Will you really come back,
Or am I only wasting my time?
What shall I do?
I hope I find the answer soon.

Don't Know What to Do

Have you somehow experienced
That you don't know what to do?
You just want to do exactly nothing
Just relax and rest the whole time?

I want to achieve something
And I feel like pursuing my dreams.
But I feel so lost and distracted
And not motivated to keep going.

I was always a risk-taker
For I never want to have any regrets.
But recently made me think
What do I really want to do?

I always question if I am on the right path
If I am indeed happy where I am.
Of what do I really want to do
And what do I really want in my life?

Even if I feel lost and tired
I still try to keep a clear mind.
To be disciplined and be grateful
To the blessings I continuously receive.

Finding time to give thanks.
Slowly building up myself.
Feeding up my soul and body.
And keep going, just keep moving.

I still don't know what to do
Not sure what is the next step to take.
I have dreams and plans in mind
Still wishing and waiting for miracles to be granted.

Anxious Mind

Deep thoughts, deep feelings,
My mind is drifting away.
Anxiously overthinking,
It is getting overwhelming.

Cannot stop myself from thinking,
Actively worrying what will happen next.
Repeating the memories again and again,
Past cycles how can I escape.

I am getting impatient,
On waiting for the right time.
If when my wish will be granted,
And start to have a better life.

Calming my mind with positive thoughts,
Clearing the negativity away.
Manifesting good things to come,
Still anxiety keeps coming back.

Trying to rest and relax,
Thinking of happy thoughts.
My anxious mind getting the best of me,
How can I fight it back?

So tired of overthinking,
Feeling helpless is worsening.
What am I to do to overcome this,
Seeking for peace within me.

My anxious mind, let's break up,
Let's start to heal and be positive.
Always have a grateful heart,
And face the day with hope and faith.

Blocked Emotions

Do you have blocked emotions?
Can I help to heal you?
Did you block me in your heart?
Will you let me into your life?

Reaching you seem so far.
Impossible to read your mind.
Confused with all your actions.
You are so unpredictable.

Will you speak your mind?
Will you show me your feelings?
Can we walk the same path together?
Can you let me heal your pain?

I want to be with you.
And I hope you will let me be.
I want to love you forever.
And spend our life together.

I know I have hurt you in the past.
And I am sincerely asking for forgiveness.
I may be the reason for your blocked heart.
For I also feel your unspoken pain.

I hope the time will come.
That you will let me heal your heart.
And put back together all the broken pieces.
To clear away your blocked emotions.

Listen to Your Heart

I keep hearing this voice within,
A silent noise yet so loud.
Listen to your heart,
Listen to your soul.

Follow your heart,
Follow your dream.
Preoccupied by earthly sounds,
Too distracted to listen.

What am I to follow?
How can I silence the noise?
Busy on searching my path,
Still feeling so lost.

One day I am stepping forward,
Then the next day I am taking a step backward.
Repeating cycles keep on happening,
When will I reach the ending?

Feeling restless and overwhelmed,
Hoping to reach the finish line.
How to listen to my heart?
Where can I find the way?

Searching for clarity,
Waiting for the answer.
Hoping for light to show up,
To guide me to the right path.

May all the noise that surrounds me stops,
And I can clearly listen to my heart's desires.
To ignite the fire and love within,
And to follow the path I am guided with.

Worth the Wait?

It has been several years
Since we had been apart.
Still until now I am not sure
On which path shall I take.

Am I still waiting on you
Or am I just holding on?
To our past memories
That made me feel comfortable.

Are we really meant to be
Back to each other's arms?
Am I only hoping for
An impossible dream?

You asked me to be patient
And not to worry too much.
To wait for you
For you need time to heal.

But why I do feel
That you are pushing me away?
You blocked me
And hurt me several times.

Are you really worth the wait
And is our connection worth fighting for?
Will you really return
To keep and fulfill your promises?

Will I really wait for you
Or shall I welcome a new beginning?
Is our past worth to rekindle
For me to patiently wait for you?

Trying to listen to my heart
But I feel too distracted.
Trying to focus on myself
But my mind keeps going back to you.

One More Chance

Have you ever been given another chance in life?
A second chance to live.
One more chance to find happiness.
Another opportunity to pursue your passion.

Do you want a second chance in love?
Will you take the offer if it will be given to you?
Or you will walk away and run as fast as you can to
avoid it?
Rather than facing it to find clarity?

Live the life you always wanted.
Sing those songs until you are out of breath.
Dance until your shoes get worn out.
Walk a thousand miles to stay grounded.

Smile to strangers you encounter daily.
Offer a helping hand to those in need.
Share your blessings with your loved ones.
Play like a kid with an innocent heart.

Sometimes you will be forced to step back,
Take it and have a break.
But do not stop there,
Regain your power and strength.

And when you feel you are ready,
Move your step forward.
Take one more chance,
To achieve that dream you always wanted.

If Meant to Be

If things are meant to be,
Then they will be.
No obstacles can stop it,
No matter what happens.

If things are meant to be,
You don't have to force it.
May take a little bit of time,
And patience may be tested.

If that dream is meant to be yours,
Your hard work will be paid off someday.
Keep thriving and keep working,
One day you will see your progress.

If that happiness is meant to be yours,
You don't have to worry and be anxious.
Stay grounded and full of positive energy,
And fill your soul with gratitude.

If that love is meant for you,
Keep your faith and it will be yours.
Your souls will find each way back,
To reunite and to be with each other forever.

If whatever is meant to be yours
Believe that they will be yours.
It may take time to reach you.
But someday they will be yours.

Unsent Message

Hey, it's me…
How are you?
Hope you are doing well…
Here I am again thinking of you.

I wanted to talk to you but could not.
Typing a message that I will delete later before
sending.
Want to tell you how much I care.
But I am too afraid to tell them.

I cannot find the courage.
I cannot find the confidence.
I miss you terribly.
That you are always in my mind.

We went separately but I am still holding on.
I could not let go of you even if I kept trying.
You have been a part of me and will always be.
Feeling like I lost a piece of me.

No matter how hard I tried to put my life together.
Something is still missing.
I really want to talk to you.
I really want to see you.

What am I supposed to do?
Here I am again thinking about you.
Wondering if I should initiate contact with you.
Shall I send a message?

Cherished Memories

You will always belong to my cherished memories.
The past we shared together.
All the good times and bad times.
All the laughter and tears.

You gave me memories to look back on.
That made me smile or sad these days.
A love we shared that was hard to forget.
Even with several years that passed could not erase.

All the hurt that you gave after we separated.
Could not overcome my loneliness.
All that sadness I had to embrace.
Gave my forgiveness but it was too hard to forget.

I was so lost and kept looking back.
Even if deep within I had to move forward.
Still hoping that we will cross our paths.
And continue the past that we started.

How can I forget my cherished memories?
If it helps me to build who I am today.
How can I forget the man I once loved.
Who taught me to explore an unknown feeling.

We don't know what our future will be.
If we will still meet again.
But our past was already part of our lives.
Cherished memories saved in our hearts.

Just Keep Showing Up

When you feel unmotivated,
And don't know what to do,
Just keep showing up,
Just keep your body moving.

Don't stay stuck in one place,
Look for opportunities ahead,
Just keep showing up,
Just keep going forward.

When you feel so down and lonely,
And feel no one there for you,
Just keep showing up,
Just believe that the people who belong to you will
find you.

Don't be afraid to try new things,
This will develop you into the person you want to be,
Just keep showing up,
Just keep pushing for your own growth.

When things feel to be falling apart,
And nothing is going as planned,
Just keep showing up,
Just know that sometimes failures are redirection for
the better.

Don't ever think of giving up,
And continue to believe in yourself,
Just keep showing up,
Just keep that faith that is within you.

I Will Be Over You Someday

I will be over you someday,
But for now, let me think about you.
I will be over you one day,
But for now, let me remember our memories.

Let me share a conversation with you,
Even just in my thoughts.
Let me share with you what happened to me today,
Even if we are no longer physically together.

Do you know that I really miss you,
Not even a single day I never think of you?
Even if you are not here feels you are here,
How am I supposed to let you go?

I will be over you, I hope so one day.
Just thinking about this makes me sad.
How can I be over you?
How can I forget you for good?

I let you go for I thought that was the best for us at
that time.
I was overwhelmed with my responsibilities,
And felt like we still had dreams to chase.
Too young for us to settle for a serious commitment.

Do I regret leaving you at that time?
I will admit I am not.
Not because I don't love you,
But because I love to see you grow.

I love to see you succeed,
And live the life you always wanted.
That time I felt I would not be of any help,
And would only pull you away from your dreams.

Now I still could not find that courage,
Could not even communicate clearly.
I will be over you someday,
But deep inside I hope it is still not over yet.

Rock Bottom

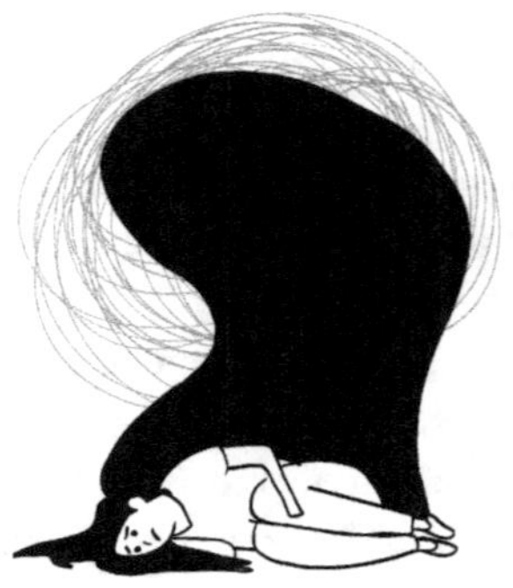

I was at my rock bottom,
Not just once but several times.
The place I never thought,
I myself would experience.

During my younger years,
I felt I was always covered by,
With all the love and support,
From my dearest and loved ones.

Feeling I always have them to lean on,
Whenever I feel I need to.
The wind beneath my wings,
The strength that pushes me through.

But as I grew up, things changed.
The persons I had looked up to,
Were not the same as I thought of.
Masks had fallen, real faces were revealed.

The people I thought were my strengths,
Were the same people as my weaknesses.
Reasons that pulled me to my rock bottom,
But I could not let go and leave.

For several years I fought to be free,
To get out of this miserable state.
When I felt I was doing well,
I was pulled back to the bottom again.

Maybe it was only my perception,
Even I blamed myself for these happenings.
And when I felt too weak and tired,
I kneeled to my knees.

Praying and hoping for help.
Asking for more strength and guidance.
To keep me going.
And to give me hope.

That someday I will be okay.
That I will get out here from the rock bottom.
To reach the top not just alone,
But together with my loved ones.

One Step at A Time

Take one step at a time
One day you will be there.
Take it slowly but steadily
Surely you will reach the end.

Take one step at a time
Even if you have to tiptoe.
Take the smallest step if you must
But keep going, keep moving.

Take one step at a time
One day you will be halfway there.
Take rest once in a while
When you feel tired and overwhelmed.

Take one step at a time
And keep the fire burning within yourself.
Take that leap of faith
And see your progress each day.

Take one step at a time
Don't stop and keep pushing.
Take care of yourself
That is the most important step.

Take one step at a time
And always have a grateful heart.
Take a deep breath to appreciate
All the blessings that surround you.

She Had Been Through Enough

She had to let you go.
She had been through enough.
She had to let go of the feeling she had for you.
She had to, even if it hurt her too.

She had to stop admiring you, adoring you,
And even loving you with her whole heart.
She was tired of all the mixed signals you gave her.
She had to, because she could not take it anymore.

She was tired of staying up all night,
Wondering what she did wrong.
Did she deserve this from someone,
When she was not the only one who made mistakes.

She was tired of listening to sad songs,
And weeping the tears endlessly.
She was tired of all the nonsense conversations,
That kept happening once in a while.

She was tired of being just the girl,
Whom you'd talked to when you felt alone.
She was tired of your selfish ways,
Not empathizing on what would be good for her too.

She had to let you go now,
And looked after herself too.
Even if she was still in love with you deeply,
What she had been through was enough.

She Chose to Live Her Life Than to Worry

She used to worry about everything.
She used to be a people pleaser.
She felt worried about upsetting others.
She felt guilty to fulfill her desires.

She got anxious about all her actions.
She got sad when something bad happened.
She was not at ease when things didn't turn out as planned.
She was not happy when things were not perfect.

Then suddenly things changed.
She hit the rock bottom she never imagined to happen.
She almost lost everything that she had.
She had experienced having her second life.

All of a sudden, realization hits her.
That in an instant, all you have can be taken away.
She needed to make the most out of life.
She needed to really start living her life.

That was when she decided to live her life to the
fullest.
To stop worrying and just let go with the flow.
Though she still had days that she felt anxious.
And need constant reminders to not be worried.

Her life is not perfect, but not the worst either.
She may not be financially rich and wealthy,
But she has a lot of blessings to be thankful for.
And she is working hard to achieve her dreams.

She is silently praying and waiting.
For the day that her dreams will be fulfilled.
But for now she is happy and content.
She chose to live her life and not to worry.

Heal Your Heart

Heal your heart, heal your soul.
Deal with your heartaches.
Heal your heart, hear your voice.
Deal with your painful feelings.

Healing may take a while.
Sometimes you feel like you want to avoid the world.
Healing is a long process.
You need to take it easy.

Heal your heart patiently.
It will be an overwhelming feeling.
Heal your heart for the better.
Keep your mind also in check.

Healing is saying no if you have to.
Some days you want to be alone too.
Healing requires support and understanding.
Do not be scared to seek help.

Heal your heart until you feel you are okay.
Achieve to have a peaceful mind and soul.
Heal your heart, heal your body.
Spend time to love and nurture yourself.

Genuine Forgiveness

How to really forgive?
How do you feel if it is genuine?
These are the questions that I asked myself several
times,
But until now I could not find the answer.

I had forgiven him and not only once,
However deep inside I feel something is still missing.
I could not find the peace,
I could not feel the contentment.

Somehow there is something,
I am still waiting for to happen.
My heart is still not at peace,
My mind actively overthinks.

They said to forgive myself,
For my past mistakes I had made.
How to truly ask for forgiveness,
When I am not sure what I am asking for?

I was told to give my genuine forgiveness,
To accept what happened in the past.
But do not forget the lessons learned,
Clear communication is a must.

Forgiveness is truly a hard work,
And not easily solved overnight.
Forgiveness requires you to earn,
Someone's trust and respect.

I am continuously praying for one day,
That I can genuinely give my forgiveness,
To myself and to others that hurt me in the past,
That I finally can let go and set myself free.

I Am Where I Am, And It's Okay

I am where I am, and it's okay.
I am surrounded by blessings.
I have a family who loves me.
I have people around that support me.

It's okay where I am now,
Though I know it's not yet my final destination.
It's a sweet spot where I feel,
I am being prepared for a better future.

Maybe my path is different from others,
Have slower progress than most,
That can be seen in the surface,
But a little step is still a progress.

Looking back for several years
Or even just a year ago,
I am proud to see my achievements
And changes to make myself better.

The lessons I learned throughout the years,
All the hardships I embraced and overcame,
All the sad and joyful tears I shed,
I am happy and proud of where I am now.

And I accepted I am still a work in progress,
Still a lot to learn and to grow,
Believing God has the best plan,
For my life and my future.

Disappointments and sadness are part of our life.
We still have a lot to be thankful and grateful for.
I am where I am, and it's okay.
And I still believe the best is yet to come.

Beyond Your Wildest Dream

What is your wildest dream?
Let me share mine with you.
Since I was a kid,
I dream to be with my soulmate one day.

To share a one true love,
To have a happily ever after,
To live in a home full of love,
To build a happy family together.

Then growing up made me realize,
This dream is not easy to achieve.
Life in reality is not like a fairy tale,
Or like a love story in the movies.

Real love is full of ups and downs,
We have a lot of imperfections,
There are distractions along the way,
Setbacks and redirections are normal.

We had other dreams to fulfill too,
Like our career and financial goals.
We have family, friends, and colleagues,
They care and love us too.

Life is more of learning how to love,
The most important person in our life,
The person that we always think of last,
And that person is us.

Life is not only about finding our soulmate.
We need to love ourselves first.
To be able to attract the person that is meant for us.
And to receive beyond our wildest dreams.

Let Go and Break Free

Let go and surrender,
Break free and live.
Let go of limiting beliefs,
Break free from your fears.

Let go of your past that holding you up,
Break free from memories that make you sad.
Let go of your unbelievable expectations,
Break free from your perfect mindset.

Let go and break free,
Follow your dreams and passions.
Let go and break free,
Listen to your heart's desires.

Let go and break free,
You are the key to your success.
Let go and break free,
Believe that you will reach your goal.

Letting go is a long process.
Breaking free is not an easy way.
Letting go will test your patience.
Breaking free will test your strength.

Still continue on letting go,
Find ways on how you will break free.
Let go and let God guide you.
Break free until your breakthrough.

Wait Patiently

Waiting patiently…
But the clock is continuously ticking.
Waiting patiently…
But time keeps on going.

Where does the time go?
Can we stop it for a little bit?
How does time run that quickly?
Why do I feel my life stops for a while?

Am I really waiting for a brighter future,
Or am I hopelessly waiting for nothing?
Am I really able to receive the blessings I deserve,
Shall I believe that dreams do really come true?

Hoping for miracles to knock in my door,
Opening my windows to welcome prosperity.
Hoping for grace and solitude,
Opening my heart to show gratitude.

Wait patiently…
A reminder I always see and hear.
Wait patiently…
A message I always receive.

New Beginnings

Don't be afraid to get out of your comfort zone.
Don't be afraid to chase your dreams.
Do not settle on what feels comfortable.
Do not settle for less than you deserve.

It is scary to welcome a new beginning,
Facing your fears and the unknown.
Challenges will be there to test you,
Keep the faith and believe in yourself.

Questioning my own abilities,
Can I really do it?
Doubting my own strengths,
Will I pursue it?

New beginnings, exciting surprises.
Unexpected changes, never-ending cycles.
Hold tight to your faith, little one.
For brighter days is just around the corner.

Unconditional Love

What is love?
How do you know if you are really in love?
What is love?
How to love someone unconditionally?

They said love is blind,
Maybe because we love beyond what our eyes can
see.
They said love is sweet,
Probably because we show affection even beyond our
expectations.

Love is not perfect,
Loving someone shows us our weakness.
Love is not selfish,
Learning to share and give care to others.

Loving unconditionally challenges our conditions,
We outweigh what we feel is important.
Loving unconditionally teaches us,
Learning lessons for us to live wiser.

Until now I ask how to love unconditionally.
I used to please people always and when needed.
Only to realize to the point I forgot about myself.
And that was when I started my journey of loving
myself unconditionally.

Live Without Regrets

Live a life without regrets,
Choose to live your life fully.
Fill your life with memories,
Find your own happiness.

Dive to your deepest desires.
Fly to your wildest dreams.
Run towards your future goals.
Drive fast to unknown destinations.

Share your precious smiles.
Walk with an open heart.
Lend your helping hands.
Breathe some fresh air.

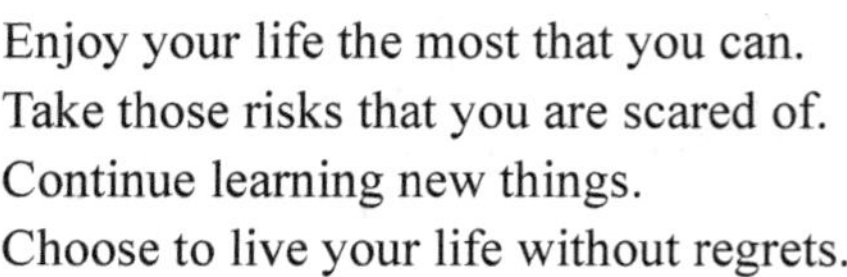

Dance with the tune of the music.
Sing those old love songs.
Cry with sad movie scenes.
Laugh on those funny jokes.

Enjoy your life the most that you can.
Take those risks that you are scared of.
Continue learning new things.
Choose to live your life without regrets.

Those Little Things

Getting separated from someone,
Made you realize the importance,
Of those little things and ways,
That we normally take for granted.

The good morning message that wakes you,
A special meal prepared for you,
Your daily afternoon walks,
Those dined out to avoid you cooking.

The long drives to take off your boredom,
Opening the car's door to get you in or out,
Lending a hand on your grocery shopping,
Choosing movies for you to watch.

Helping you do the house chores,
Making your morning coffee,
Spending time with family and friends,
Making efforts to meet your expectations.

Those little things that now gone,
Only stay forever in our memories.
Will they still happen again?
Who knows what our future holds.

Like A Diamond

Sparkling through the lights,
Captivating enormous attention.
Showing elegant style,
Beauty standing out from the crowd.

Worth shines through the eyes,
Still wanted by many.
Regardless of the value,
Anyone gravitated by its rarity.

Just like a diamond,
That was formed from heat and pressure,
Developed by billions of times,
Started from darkness to shine.

Believe that all your progress,
Is building you for the day,
That you will outshine your beauty,
Just like how a diamond can.

Be confident that the time will come,
That all your hard work and patience,
Will showcase your power and creativity,
For the world to see and experience.

Lost Opportunity

You almost had it
Just a few chances away.
You almost got it
Still it was out of reach.

In a glimpse of an eye
You lost the opportunity.
In a matter of seconds
You had lost the chance.

Step back and relax
Refresh your perspective.
Look outside the box
Search for new opportunities.

It is not the end of the road
Reroute and enjoy the ride.
Experience exciting memories
Learn and enhance your capabilities.

See lost opportunities as blessings
A better way to improve yourself.
To seek unexplored knowledge
That guides us to our real journey.

Karma

Right or wrong,
We get what we deserve.
We will get served,
What is rightfully ours.

What goes around comes around,
And we cannot avoid it.
That is why we must think first,
Before we act and react.

We will reap what we sow,
Be careful what you are planting.
One day the fruit of your actions,
Will land in your hands.

Karma is real,
And we shall believe it.
Whether it is good or bad,
It is for our own sake.

Time is gold and the clock is ticking.
Choose to keep doing good,
And always set good intentions,
It will come back to you in unexpected ways.

Right Directions

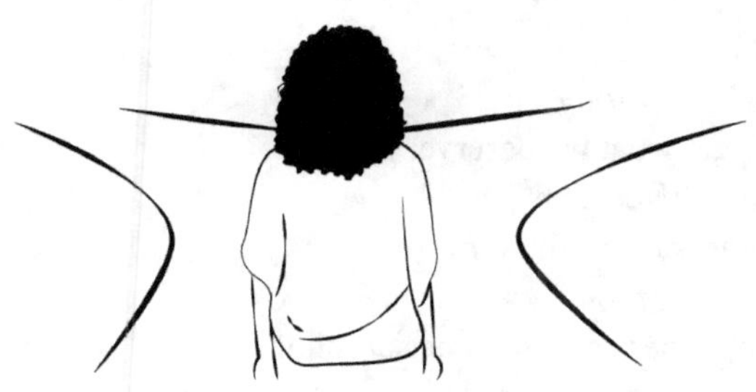

Stumbling with my own feet,
Feeling lost and distracted.
Could not find my way,
Could not find my will to keep going.

Losing my momentum,
Losing my faith.
Feeling weary and weak.
Stressing with anxious thoughts.

Searching for the right direction,
Navigating through darkness.
Walking in diversities,
Embracing kindness.

Using my heart as a compass,
I believe I will find my path.
Will keep on moving,
And seek the right direction.

How I wish I Can

How I wish I can…
Send you a message to say hello.
How I wish I can…
Call you when I want to hear your voice.

How I wish I can…
Walk with you to enjoy the sun.
How I wish I can…
Sit on the passenger seat while you drive.

How I wish I can…
Have your first greeting in the morning.
How I wish I can…
Eat a meal that you especially prepare for me.

How I wish I can…
Celebrate your special moments.
How I wish I can…
Be part of your daily routine.

How I wish I can…
Share your future dreams.
How I wish I can…
Help you heal when you are in pain.

How I wish I can…
Be your partner and stay forever.
How I wish I can…
Make this wish happen in reality.

Love Yourself

Embrace your own beauty,
Love your own body.
Embrace your imperfections,
Love yourself fully as you are.

Have you seen your reflection,
Are you happy with what you see?
Have you seen the shine in your eyes,
That shows your inner beauty?

Love yourself as you have always loved others,
Show yourself the same respect.
Love yourself that you deserve for your own
happiness,
For you to be able to share your love unconditionally.

Be compassionate with yourself,
And cherish your own feelings.
Choose to follow your dreams,
And listen to the desires of your heart.

Love yourself first and always,
It is not selfish but necessary.
Learn to love yourself no matter what,
For you to be able to share your love gracefully.

Magnetic Attraction

Have you been so attracted to someone,
That feels like something gravitating you,
Towards someone very strongly,
Pulling you like with a magnetic force?

Sounds magical and ironic,
And does not make sense as well,
However no reasoning can answer,
All these questions in my head.

Had been in this situation for a while now,
Seems I cannot get myself out of,
Cycles just keep on repeating,
Chasing a relationship with no end.

Why I have this strong feeling for someone,
Hoping I will find clarity?
Why I am still interested in someone,
Hoping I will find the answer too?

Answer arriving and I will keep the faith,
Praying for a positive outcome,
Manifesting a miracle in love,
With magnetic force interaction.

Stop Comparing Yourself

Stop comparing yourself to others,
You are not in competition with anyone.
Stop comparing yourself to someone,
You are a unique individual as you are.

Stop comparing yourself to the person next to you,
You are both beautiful in different ways.
Stop comparing yourself to her,
You are not her and she is not you.

Compare yourself to your past self,
Do you see all your improvements?
Compare yourself from a year ago,
Do you feel proud of yourself?

Compare yourself constantly,
To the past version of yourself.
Stop comparing yourself to others,
You are not on the same journey.

Am I Over You?

Am I over you,
Or am I only faking it?
Am I over you,
Then why am I still stuck on you?

Is moving on a long process?
If it is, then how long?
Is leaving behind this painful?
Why do I still feel you in my life?

All I wish is the best for you,
Even if I am not a part of it.
All I want is for you to be happy,
Even if we are on separate ways.

But why am I still holding on,
To the promise you made in the past?
Why am I still waiting,
For you to come back someday?

We Don't Know

We don't know what we don't know,
And we know what we know.
We don't need to know what we don't know,
But we need to know what we need to know.

You know what you do,
And that is all that matters.
You need to know what to do,
And it is up to you to take action.

Amusing to see as things get revealed,
When you knowingly knew,
The things that yet to be discovered,
Watching as the truth sheds its own light.

You can keep what we don't know,
But until when you can hold the silence?
Time has its own unexpected ways,
On revealing our deepest secrets.

Divine Timing

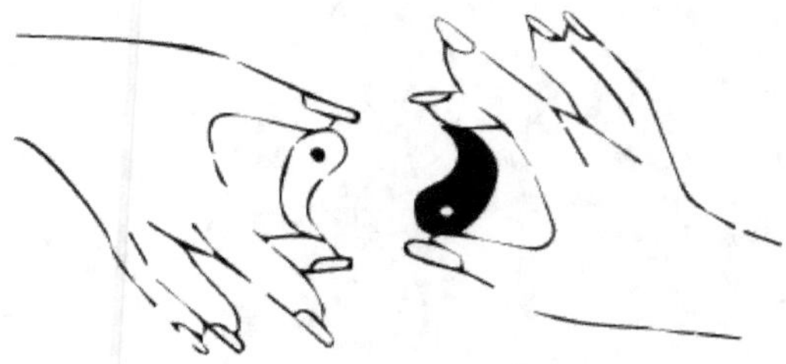

It made me question most of the time
The power of divine timing.
Not because I don't believe on it
But it made me test my patience.

Every time I made a reckless move
It only made the situation worse.
Rather than helping to clear the path
It felt like I had to step back again from the start.

This made me think wisely
All the decisions I had to make.
I want my plan to succeed
And not to fail and to retreat.

I am highly manifesting a dream
Until now I am still patiently waiting.
For the divine timing to happen
And give me the green light to proceed.

Unfold Naturally

Get out of your head,
Live in the moment.
Let things unfold naturally,
Stop controlling the outcome.

Breathe and relax,
They will unfold naturally.
Look and step back,
Everything is going to be okay.

Do not force the process,
Like how nature unfolds naturally.
The flowers waiting to bloom,
And fruits waiting to get ripe.

Just wait patiently,
It will be worth it in the end.
Let the universe take the
lead,
And wait for the time to
unfold naturally.

With Gratitude

Tonight my knees got shaken again,
Hearing those deafening alarms,
Made me reminded of those,
Frightening and weakening moments.

I am grateful that we are all safe,
No harm happened,
I am grateful that those were alarms only,
And not another tragedy.

Thank you God,
From the bottom of my heart,
Thank you for protection,
And calming my weariness.

Thank you God,
For sending your angels to guard us.
Thank you universe,
For giving us comfort.

I am truly grateful,
And continuously praying,
To keep us all safe,
And protected from all harm.

And I Waited

And I waited…
And still waiting…
Though honestly I don't know,
What I am really waiting for.

Is this waiting…
Will all be worth it in the end?
Is this waiting…
Worth the time I am wasting?

Will you really return
And keep your promise?
Will you come back
For us to reunite?

Yes I am still waiting…
And trying to be patient.
Yes I am still waiting…
And fighting all my fears.

I will still wait for you,
Even if this journey takes a longer time.
I will still wait for you,
Until you find your way home.

Wishing I Am Near Your Side

One of those nights again,
I am really missing my parents,
I am missing my family,
I am missing my loved ones.

How I wish we didn't have this long distance.
How I wish I could come to you whenever I want to.
How I wish I were not living this far.
How I wish I were not living alone far from all of
you.

At first I had to chase my dreams.
Then a certain circumstance made me choose to stay
far away.

I had to sacrifice for our family's future.
I had to give away my own dream.

I had to fight all this sadness.
I had to be brave and learn to be strong.
I could not give up even if I were tired.
I had to hide my tears and show my smiles.

My only wish is to be able to close the gap,
That I can see you all from time to time.
That I can spend a little bit of time,
To be with you all once in a while.

I really wish to come home.
I really wish to be near you all.
I really wish I could make it.
I really wish it to happen in the near future.

Treat Yourself Better

How are you feeling?
Are you treating yourself better?
Do you prioritize yourself above others?
Are you taking care of yourself?

Self-care is essential, it is not selfish.
You have to give yourself love,
So that you can share your love with others.
Give love to yourself unconditionally.

What is the thing you want to do the most?
Do it and spend time with yourself.
It does not need to be grand,
Those little moments are worthwhile.

Treat yourself better,
Same as how you treat others.
Treat yourself better,
Same as how you want to be treated.

Love yourself, treat yourself.
Don't feel guilty and bad about it.
Glow and shine your happiness.
Be yourself and others will follow.

You've Got This

In a world full of expectations
…you've got this!
In times you feel unsure
…you've got this!

What I am trying to say is…
You can do whatever is in your mind.
What I mean is…
You can be the best person you want to be.

You have to believe in yourself.
You have to step up the game.
Small steps are all that matters.
Making the first move is all that counts.

You've got this, and I know you can!
I will be your best cheerleader.
You've got this, you can make it.
And I will see you at the final destiny.

Speak Your Mind

Speak your mind,
Share your thoughts.
Show those brilliant ideas,
Say your inspiring stories.

Have freedom with your words,
Don't limit your imagination.
Be brave with your abilities.
Be worthy of your knowledge.

The world will listen,
Let your mind speak.
The world will hear,
Be creative of your words.

Share your wisdom,
Be passionate about your work.
Speak up your mind,
Let your heart lead the way.

Hope I Know

Hope I know what is going on,
Wish I knew what was happening.
Hope I have a way to know,
Wish I had the right to know.

When things are being hidden from you,
When you lose the ability to control.
How these things happen,
How to get those back?

You know you are being protected,
And you know you are being guided.
Even if you walk blindly,
And even if your path is not clear.

Still you hope you know what is happening,
You have an idea of what will happen next.
You know you have to keep your trust for a better
future,
And hold your patience with utmost faith.

Are You Ready?

Can you feel it?
Are you ready?
Can you perceive it?
Are you excited?

Those things you continuously manifest,
May soon arrive.
Those things you deeply dream,
May soon come true.

Are you ready for it?
Prepare yourself to claim it.
Are you happy about it?
You deserve it gracefully.

Finally the time you patiently wait,
Is eventually coming to fruition.
Finally all those hard work,
Is ultimately paying off handsomely.

Are you ready?
You better be.
Get ready for the blessings to come.
Claim it gratefully with open arms.

Limiting Beliefs

Test your limits
Try new ideas
Stretch your boundaries
Do things you never think you can.

Go for a long drive
Climb that mountain
Book that ticket to the concert
Treat yourself to a movie.

Go to that fancy restaurant
Buy that precious gift
Try new outfits
Get those sets of shoes.

Buy yourself those flowers
Treat yourself in a date
Travel to those destinations
Get your body fit and healthy.

Test your limiting beliefs
Do those things to make yourself better
Start it now even if only by yourself
For it is the best time to do it.

Opposites Attract

Two different individuals,
With two different personalities.
Two people you never thought,
That one day destined to meet.

Had opposite ideas about life,
Choose opposite decisions.
Going in different directions,
But fate made them meet halfway.

A destiny you cannot avoid,
An attraction difficult to deny.
So strong and powerful,
A love so rare to find.

When two opposites attract,
It will be unstoppable.
Adding the divine intervention,
Love surely will conquer and win in the end.

When Things Start to Fall Into Place

Why am I here in this darkness?
I want to get outside.
Why does it feel like everything is falling apart?
I want to be free.

All I want is peace,
All I want is to be happy.
Why is it so difficult to find?
Why does it feel out of reach?

Praying for a better tomorrow,
Hoping for better days.
Striving for more opportunities
Trying to be more optimistic.

Are things really starting to,
Fall into its rightful places?
Are things really happening,
For what is best for my highest self?

Searching for light through the dark.
Lifting my head when I feel discouraged.
Keeping all faith within my heart.
Believing things falling into their right places.

You Are Enough

You are enough, you are worth it.
You are powerful, you are strong.
You are beautiful inside and out.
You are perfect just the way you are.

You are enough, just because.
You are enough, and so do I.
You can be who you want to be.
You can do whatever you want to do.

You don't have to feel guilty.
You have all the right to be happy.
You don't have to play small.
You can chase up those impossible dreams.

You are important no matter what.
You are special in this life.
You know how to love.
You deserve to be loved.

You are enough for who you are.
You are enough for anyone to have.
You just need to be yourself.
You must believe you are enough.

Invisible String Attached

Can you feel our connection
That binds me towards you?
Maybe because of the invisible string
That attaches us together.

I tried to forget you,
But I keep on coming back.
I am so drawn to you,
Too hard to let you go.

My mind said to move forward,
And never try to look back.
But my heart yearns for you,
That I keep on returning to you.

One step forward today,
Two steps backward the next day.
Seems difficult to progress,
Had to take a different route.

I tried to cut this cord attached to us,
But it was unbreakable.
My feelings just got stronger,
And made me want you more.

This invisible string attaching us,
Made me believe in forever.
Even if we have our separate ways now,
We can find each other again one day.

Lead Me The Way

Lead me the way God,
Please don't let me go astray.
Send your angels to guide me,
Please protect me from evil.

Lead me the way to my purpose,
Please don't let me lose sight of it.
Show me the right directions,
Please send me your grace.

Lead me the way to be grateful,
To be thankful for the blessings I received.
Let me be mindful to the needs of others,
Share kindness towards humanity.

Lead me the way to you God,
Let me show love to others.
To be a way to help the people in need,
And be your faithful servant.

Just Because

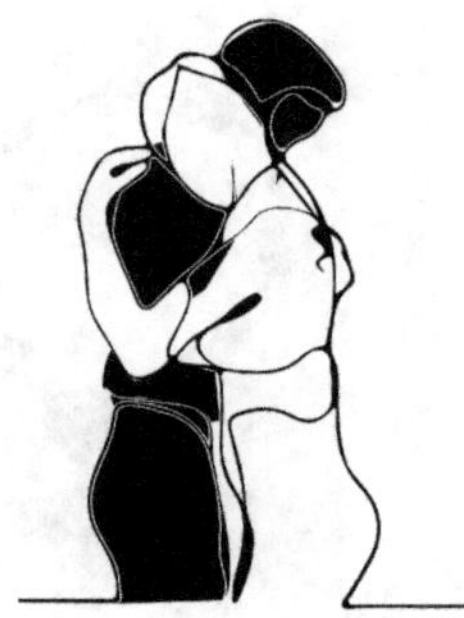

Just because, no other excuse.
Or shall I mean,
I don't know what to say.

Just because, nothing more.
Just think about what,
I really meant to say.

Just because, don't overthink.
I don't know how to explain,
What I really do feel.

Just because, I like you.
You intrigued me to the core.
You had attracted my interest.

Just because, I love you too.
That's all I want to say.
A reason that makes me happy.

Open Your Heart

Open your heart to receive,
Don't stop your own blessings.
Open your heart to love,
Feel that happiness in your life.

Open your heart to receive,
You deserve those praises.
Believe you are a wonderful human being,
Worthy of all those blessings.

Open your eyes to see the light,
That shines brightly to lead your path.
Open your eyes to see the beauty,
Appreciate all these that surround you.

Open your heart to receive,
For all the love your loved ones offer.
Accept all the kindness they give.
Show gratitude for their sacrifices.

Open your heart to receive,
Listen to that little voice inside you.
Believe that the love you always dream,
Is on the way to your heart soon.

Breaking to Breakthrough

My heart had to be broken to seek through the light.
Had to get lost to search for the right path.
My heart had to be broken to learn how to love.
Had to endure breaking for a breakthrough.

Breaking free of what I keep silently inside of me.
Speaking up what is on my mind.
Breaking the barriers to reach my dreams.
Trying to break free in a better and positive way.

Never knew how to live until I had fallen.
Had taken advantage of life and did not know how to
appreciate it.
Never know how to love until I've lost it.
Now I keep on chasing it and still cannot find it.

For us to reach our desired destination,
Breakups and disappointments are to happen.
For us to realize what we truly desire,
We had to meet and pass several lessons in life.

It will be a long and lonely journey,
That will question your worthiness.
But believe that you deserve the best.
These breakings will lead you to your breakthrough.

www.ingramcontent.com/pod-product-compliance
Lightning Source LLC
LaVergne TN
LVHW011044200726
843509LV00011B/1349